Dedication

This Book of Hope is dedicated to individuals and families around the world who have gone through, or are going through, the storms of life.

Though these events are hard to accept, understand and move beyond, perhaps the words of this book will offer you and those you love, comfort, peace, encouragement, healing, wisdom, inspiration and, above all, Hope.

My prayer is, "May the God of Hope fill each of you abundantly, with Divine peace, joy, faith and hope that overflows into every life you touch."

Presented to

_____

From

_____

Date

_____

By Cecil O. Kemp, Jr.

Edited by Kathryn Knight

Art Direction and Design by Anderson Thomas Design, Nashville, Tennessee

The Wisdom Company, Inc.

P.O. Box 681351, Franklin, TN 37068-1351 1-800-728-1145

A BOOK OF HOPE

for

the Storms of Life

HEALING WORDS FOR TROUBLED TIMES

ABOUT THE HOPE COLLECTION AND ITS CREATOR

The Hope Collection books are based on the message of Real Hope shared in Cecil O. Kem Jr.'s acclaimed inspirational book, *Wisdom Honor & Hope (The Inner Path to True Greatness).*

Hope —

without it, no one can live very long.
No great conquests have ever been won
   without it.
No one has ever seen better days without
   hoping for them.
Nurture hope and it will reward you.
Hope is the sunshine of life and the angel
   that puts a song in your heart.

Hope sings its song one heart at a time.
Hope lifts you and sustains you and at the
   same time lifts and sustains others.
Tucked deep in our heart, Hope renews the
   soul and gets us through life's storms.
Hope comes like a prayer from God,
   reminding the heart of its higher
   purpose and dreams.

WHAT GIVES YOU HOPE?

We invite readers to begin their own journey of the heart toward real and lasting peace, hope happiness and success.

Cecil O. Kemp, Jr. lived his dream, becoming a successful businessman and business owner. Yet, he was very unfulfilled. Enormous material success didn't deliver on its promises of hope and happiness. He set out to discover the secrets of a genuinely happy, hopeful life. Finding and applying them, he freed himself and his family from the rat race life, while enjoying even greater material success. After nearly two decades of this higher prosperity, he and his fellow writing friends offer those amazing discoveries in The Hope Collection.

Special Thanks

As you soak in the beauty, power and warmth of this and other Hope Collection books, remember these are the work of some very talented, special people. Special thanks to Anderson Thomas Design, Wes Yoder and Ron Miller at Ambassador Agency, Stephen von Hagel, Brenda McClearen and Robert Keifer.

Introduction

Life is not a bed of roses. We are not promised freedom from sorrow, pain, or hardship. The reality of fast-paced modern society is that storms blow through lives every single day. Loss of loved ones, near fatal accidents, severe health problems and personal, financial and on the job setbacks, all overwhelm us with fears. As storms snowball, they wreck our emotions, spirits, relationships, homes, and organizations. In their wake, it is not uncommon for people to freeze in place, lose hope, give up or drop out of the mainstream. Just as often, they move forward at less than 100% spiritually, emotionally, physically and fiscally.

Author Cecil O. Kemp, Jr. has experienced life's storms and the tears, fears, and sorrow that go with them. His inner inspection, introspection and search for meaning and answers led Cecil to discover what he calls *The Inner Path to True Greatness*. He turned onto the time-tested road that leads from lowest lows to the highest high and has helped many others do the same.

He helps us confront the two most important questions faced, when storms land in our lives:

> OUT OF THE LOWEST DEPTHS THERE IS A PATH TO THE LOFTIEST HEIGHT.
> —*Thomas Carlyle*

Where do you turn, faced with broken dreams, lives or relationships, the death of a loved one, financial disaster, or serious health problems?

Where does your strength come from?

Truth is, many of us get angry and make life "hell on earth", for others and ourselves. Others just ignore difficulties, hoping they will go away. Neither approach leads to good answers or lasting healing, hope and growth.

Cecil is emphatic that troubled times are the opportunities for greatest growth. But in compassionate, comforting, and healing words of wisdom and peace, he shares how to discover seeds of Real Hope within tears that spill out of bruised and broken hearts. He encourages and lifts us with the assurances that tears clear vision, bathe the soul and gracefully dance back into our eyes, down into our soul, becoming precious, heart-held memories and seeds of future hope. He inspires and promises each that The Inner Path to True Greatness is where Real Hope is found.

If you have been hurt, bruised, and left disillusioned by the storms, tragedies and losses of life, go with him now on a journey to a place called Hope where your spirit can be renewed, your dreams and faith restored and your life changed, so that you become and achieve everything God intended at the moment He created you.

NUGGET OF HOPE

The Inner Path to True Greatness is a chosen walk through life–traveled by those who allow Divinely inspired faith and vision to help them grow, mature, and fulfill their highest purpose and destiny.

PART ONE

You will understand.

BE NOT AFRAID OF
LIFE. BELIEVE THAT
LIFE IS WORTH
LIVING, AND YOUR
BELIEF WILL HELP
CREATE THE FACT.

—William James

You can get through!

I heard a whisper behind closed doors
the simple words uttered were blessed and pure
and something happened that miraculous day
when I heard a child pray

Sparrows gathered on the window sill
and the earth's sweet chamber became quiet and still
and heaven's arms embraced oceans and hills
when I heard a child pray

Angels began dancing on the silver clouds
and nations laid down their weapons and quietly bowed
And the souls that had been lost were suddenly found
When I heard a child pray

Something miraculous happened that day
in the heart of a child the Lord came to stay
reminding us all in a special way
to listen... when a child prays

–*When A Child Prays*
A Poem by Debbie Guthery

YOU WILL.

YOU CAN.

YOU MUST.

Divine enlightenment can help us to eventually understand what may seem totally senseless and completely unfair. Divine Hope gives us the peace and willpower to wisely choose to step into the future, now!

Why do bad things sometimes happen to good people? Where was God, when the bad thing happened? Doesn't The Divine care?

Let's answer the last two questions, first. The Divine is always present with us in spirit. And, yes, God cares so much that you and I, members of the greatest Divine creation, were given the freedom of choice and God's unconditional love.

Now, let's answer the first question. I believe the answer lies in the God-given freedom of choice we all have. Because each of us has that liberty, good people can be terribly affected by others' unwise choices. If freedom of choice were taken from us, we would be right to point fingers skyward. But none of us wants our freedoms taken away, especially the freedom to choose.

Ann Landers says we should "expect trouble as an inevitable part of life, and, when it comes, hold your head high, look it squarely in the eye, and say, 'I will be bigger than you.'" If life's tragedies have left you confused, angry, badly bruised, and disappointed, summon every ounce of your resolve and commit yourself to stand tall and follow through on even the smallest tasks every day. Do it, even if it feels unnatural right now.

And be encouraged, knowing that, in time, The Divine mends broken hearts, dreams, lives, relationships, and families. God helps us see that to grow we must heal, and to heal, we must let go.

NUGGET OF HOPE

Choose to believe in Divine Hope, let go of the past, and leave the desert of "why," knowing that farther along you will understand. You will, you can, you must!

THERE IS HOPE.

You feel pain. You feel loss. Perhaps you even feel betrayed, angry, confused. But you do feel–and that is what tells you that your soul–your spirit–is alive and can move forward. Thank God–literally–that you feel! Thank God that you recognize and react to storms of life, things out of joint, injustice, and unkindness.

Because we cry out, either alone or collectively, against the tragedies that still befall mankind–*there is Hope.* Because we mourn those we lose needlessly–*there is Hope.* Because we express anger over war–*there is Hope.* Because we feel sorrow to our very core–*there is Hope.* With this sorrow and pain comes a reconnection to the spirit that cries out for peace. If we find that peace, with God's great help, we can change the world–one person, one spirit, at a time and this is where Real Hope begins.

Real Hope is a Divinely imbued peace and security that allows joy and conviction to reside in the Spirit-led heart–no matter the circumstances, no matter the consequences. It goes beyond optimism. It is a powerful, reassuring "knowledge" in the heart of what is Truth–and that Truth and Love are abiding. It is difficult to define yet you do know it when you are lifted by it. It is a Hope that exists beyond one's self–a

OF ALL THE FORCES THAT MAKE FOR A BETTER WORLD, NONE IS SO INDISPENSABLE, NONE SO POWERFUL, AS HOPE. WITHOUT HOPE MEN ARE HALF-ALIVE. WITH HOPE THEY THINK AND DREAM AND WORK.
–Charles Sawyer

Love from The Divine that embraces us all, even those who do not acknowledge and feel its presence. And because it is beyond us, we cannot destroy it or diminish it. It is there, it always has been. What we can do is breathe it in and partake in it. And this we do when we allow the Wisdom and Grace of God to enter our hearts.

Hope sings its song one heart at a time. We can become part of it. We can't create it—it flows from the Divine Embrace—but we can glow with it and awaken others to it. Hope is far-sighted. It sees a better tomorrow, even in the midst of chaos, sorrow and pain. It sees the good in the criminal, the reward in a "defeated" stand for justice, the worth in what is considered lowly, the potential in the arrogant and cruel, and the joy in service.

This Hope comes like a prayer from God who reminds the heart of its real dreams and passions and whispers: *It's alright. I know. I'm here. We've got work to do.* Having Real Hope is not easy or automatic. It is a choice. It is a leap of faith in today's culture. But if you leap, you are promised Divine help, guidance, wings—and Real Hope. If you leap, you are following your heart and your true destiny. If you leap you will find yourself living incredibly —walking The Inner Path to True Greatness hand in hand with God.

NUGGET OF HOPE

When Real Hope fills the heart, we begin to realize our highest destiny—truly, fully.

SELAH

Selah means pause, to deeply ponder something.

Think about your own thoughts. Realize that they are "making" you. What you think about will shape you and your destiny.

Living a life of True Greatness begins with how your heart responds to events around you, your desires, and your very thoughts.

This is why your beliefs and values must be clear in your heart and mind.

This is why a life of True Greatness must begin with Wisdom before it can become Honorable and create Hope for all others.

> YOUR THOUGHTS
> ARE MAKING YOU.
> *—Bishop Steere*

This is why St. Paul wrote to the Philippians:

NUGGET OF HOPE

Whatsoever things are true, whatsoever things are honest, whatsoever things are just, whatsoever things are pure, whatsoever things are lovely, whatsoever things are of good report; if there be any virtue and if there be any praise, think on these things.

NEW STRENGTHS & BLESSINGS

The storms of life often disguise the strengths we will discover from them and the blessings their lessons will lead us to in the future.

I challenge you to consider your past storms, failures, and successes and all you went through. Each was a learning experience that made you who you are today.

Though it may well take time before you understand today's difficulties, you can grow from them as you move into a brighter, better future.

NUGGET OF HOPE

Storms of life are opportunities to pause...

–reconnect to God, others and ourselves

–learn and grow from them

–and discover within them strengths and future blessings.

DOUBTS

Doubts in the storms of life are normal, but they are not barriers. Though they bring current discomfort and inner conflict, doubts that lead us to what I call "intellectual spiritual search leading to heartfelt change" present wonderful opportunities, from knowing and understanding ourselves, our Creator, and others better.

Toss the bridle of doubts and its fears that block your vision and courage. Put on the bridle of faith that removes your doubts and fears, restoring your higher vision and hope.

THERE LIVES MORE FAITH IN HONEST DOUBT, BELIEVE ME, THAN IN HALF THE CREEDS.
—*Alfred, Lord Tennyson*

NUGGET OF HOPE

Faith and hope are our heart's eyes and higher intellect, the spiritual vision and knowledge that drive fear from our spirit as we soar beyond doubt.

DENIAL

Denial blindfolds pain and blocks the path to progress.

It is easier to cover our eyes than it is to face our pain. Denial is the shadow of our unconfronted pain. Our resistance is rooted in fear of loss, the unknown and the future. But these are only masks of great opportunity to learn, grow and prosper.

Facing the storms of life and their pain, we can understand them better and learn the lessons embedded in them. When we recognize that pain is a source of inspiration and teacher of wisdom, we can see the dawning of a new day, one where we have the opportunity to take wise and honorable action toward a bright, far more hopeful future.

NUGGET OF HOPE

Free yourself, no need to resist, remove the mask of denial, face the pain, discover the wise lessons, and apply them as you step onto and travel the path of progress.

FEARS

Acknowledge that fears are real, then escort them to flight.

Sometimes we let our fears determine who we are, how we are supposed to be and thus, control what we do. Surrounded by fears, we run to corners and refuse to come out.

However, life is meant to be challenged and explored. Fears can motivate us to take positive, constructive actions, when we face them head-on. The inner resources to overcome fears are Wisdom, Honor, and Hope.

Recognize your fear–this is wise.
Learn from and release your fear–this is honorable.
Know that a better life awaits–this is hopeful.

NUGGET OF HOPE

Say good-bye to your fears, leap from their grasp, experience things believed, see your dreams come true and your highest hopes and aspirations become reality.

COURAGE

For those who have been spiritually reborn, courage means they are free to eliminate the excuses, leave the safety of the ledge, and fly with faith, knowing that The Divine Spirit within them will support them.

There are times in our lives when it takes courage just to survive. Harriet Beecher Stowe wrote, "When you get into a tight place, and everything goes against you, till it seems as though you could not hold on a moment longer, never give up then–for that is just the place and time that the tide will turn."

A wise person, whose heart is full of Divine Hope and Grace, keeps the faith, acts with courage, endures, helps others when they stumble or become tired, weeps with those who weep, and presses on.

Charles Beard once said, "When it is dark enough, you can see the stars." And, Jesse Jackson said, "Hold your head high, stick your chest out. You can make it. It gets dark sometimes but morning comes–Keep hope alive." We can look at the sky and choose to see either the darkness or the brightness of the stars. When we choose to look at the stars, we express our faith and courage that good will come and growth will occur in our lives and the lives of everyone we love. We can and should expect the best, walking The Inner Path to True Greatness.

When we are faced with adversity, how we handle the storm is far more important than mere survival. Courageously enduring often means pain, sweat, and tears. Life can fling its unexpected storms. Family and others can throw harsh words at us, in anger. People can engage in many other destructive behaviors that can harm us and those we love. At times, there is no good reason for what happens. How we handle these situations is what counts. The present and eternal rewards of courage and endurance are very worthwhile.

Look inside. Discover your wings of faith and take courage in them. As you stretch them and move them, aim for new heights.

NUGGET OF HOPE

The Divine within, one who has been spiritually reborn has the vision to see that no walls or ceilings confine, and the courage to use their inner wings of faith to soar safely to greater heights.

LET THE HEALING BEGIN!

Healing starts in the heart and works its way outward—to our thinking, attitudes, and then our behavior and performance.

Positive emotions and wise character are created and nurtured by a heart full of Truth, guided by the Spirit of God.

THE ONLY MEDICINE FOR SUFFERING, CRIME, AND ALL OTHER WOES OF MANKIND, IS WISDOM.
—T. H. Huxley

With The Divine Spirit inside and alongside us each day, we have the inner spiritual peace that is the wellspring of healing and wholeness.

NUGGET OF HOPE
Heart health is the wellspring of healing and wholeness.

POWER IN BELIEVING

Belief is a key to healing, recovery, renewal, and future achievement.

A trusting heart is a believing heart–one at peace, full of Real Hope. This serene scene has no place for anxiety, fear or worry.

DRUGS ARE NOT ALWAYS NECESSARY, BUT BELIEF IN RECOVERY ALWAYS IS.
–Norman Cousins

A heart full of Divine Hope is guided by wise ambition, brimming with confidence, continually moving its owner in the direction of true success.

NUGGET OF HOPE

Believe, put to work the power in believing. It gets us through difficulties of today and tomorrow and sustains our Hope of a brighter and blessed future.

THE GOOD IN GRIEVING

Loss is real and brings conflicting emotions, tears and grief. Yet, the pain of loss is a source of inspiration and teacher of wisdom.

In my crying, inner conflict, grief, and introspection following forced sale of a business built from scratch, a near fatal accident and my father's unexpected death, I experienced healing and growth.

When my father died, I was devastated. Big C was the greatest man I have ever known. No one else even comes close. At the time, I could not understand why and definitely could not envision all the

TAKE THIS SORROW TO YOUR HEART. MAKE IT A PART OF YOU. AND IT SHALL ASSURE YOU ARE STRONG AGAIN.
—Robert Longfellow

good that has come my way and to many others, as a result of his death.

But, from this storm of life, I learned that as life's burdens and pains grow, God gives us more grace and strength. With each added affliction, He adds His mercy and His multiplied peace is given, as we face more trials. Now, I know better than ever The Divine's love has no limit, His grace cannot be measured by puny human standards and His power has no boundary that we humans can understand. When we are at the end of our store of endurance, our strength failing and our resources gone, our heavenly Father's giving has only just begun and has no end, limit or boundary.

From my father, one who was truly great, I have learned to celebrate opportunity for discovery, finding joy in each new experience and cultivating hope for tomorrow, planting seeds today. Even in death, he is still teaching and inspiring me how to scale walls never faced and to jump back into the bright future, onto the path of success. Acceptance of the reality of this loss brought me new vision and served as motivation for the future.

And, I discovered how important it is to let go of everything except the good memories. Bathed in tears, the past becomes a beautiful memory the heart holds forever and the touchstone of a brighter, better future full of Hope and many possibilities. Faced with pain and loss, those who live life well choose to look up, to attain hopeful attitudes as they are filled with Divine grace, love, inspiration, strength and power, knowing hopeful action and positive, enduring results will follow.

To find comfort from pain and loss, I urge you to reach within to discover the inspiring and wise lessons embedded in those life experiences–and then use those for good, for yourself and others as you reach out to them.

NUGGET OF HOPE
Have a good cry, wash out your heart. *–From a song by Dr. Hook*

DIVINE REFUGE

In the midst of change, difficulties or success, what joy it is
to know that we can take refuge in The Divine.

No matter where we find ourselves, we can always find rest,
Hope, peace and discover new strengths—safely embraced in
the sanctuary of Divine Love.

NUGGET OF HOPE

This is well-nigh the greatest of discoveries a man can make, that God is not
confined in churches, but that the streets are sacred because His presence is
there, that the market-place is one of His abiding places, and ought, there-
fore, to be a sanctuary. Any moment in any place, the veil can suddenly grow
thin and God be seen.

—R. C. Gillie

THE POWER OF PRAYER

To know the way up and down the mountain, ask the one who made the mountain.

The life changing power of prayer is real.

Prayer and their faith give those who live well the inner Hope and power needed to live every day optimistically confident and without fear or worry of what may or may not happen.

Alone time with The Divine brings everything into proper perspective. Those who shape a special life and an eternally enduring legacy of Hope follow Jesus' profound teaching to continually turn inward to distill, reflect, evaluate—and commune, in the private inner room of the soul, with The Divine Spirit.

In prayer, meditation and study of Eternal Truth in the Bible, we connect directly to The Divine's thoughts and ways. Meditation on higher thoughts nurtures the inner life of the spirit. A vibrant inner spirit is one connected directly to The Divine. Through this connection flows peace beyond understanding that keeps the heart calm and quietly confident, even in troubled times created by the storms of life.

A sound mind grows from an untroubled heart, inspired by Divine Wisdom. Be still, rest your mind, listen to the beating of your heart, find the peace from above that is undisturbed by worry. Breathe in the peace, tranquility, strength and Hope of prayer and meditation on Eternal Truth.

William Wolford wrote, "Sweet hour of prayer! Sweet hour of prayer! That calls me from a world of care, And bids me at my Father's throne. Make all my wants and wishes known. In seasons of distress and grief, my soul has often found relief."

NUGGET OF HOPE

Prayer is an invisible tool that can make a very visible difference.

ANGELIC ASSISTANCE

When asked, The Divine dispenses special guardian angels to protect His children, ministering angels to help and care for them.

There can be no doubt there are angels among us, when we look around with an open mind and consider life through the higher vision of faith.

NUGGET OF HOPE

Angels are spirit messengers sent by The Divine to protect, help and care for the children of God. *–St. Paul*

FINDING JOY

Regardless of our circumstances, we are wise to count our blessings and to rejoice and be glad, knowing those far outweigh life's hardships.

CHEERFULNESS
GIVES ELASTICITY
TO THE SPIRIT.
–Samuel Smiles

By opening our hearts to the beauty and possibilities around us, we invite laughter, joy, peace and immense hope of a brighter, better future.

NUGGET OF HOPE

In all circumstances, it is wise and hopeful to rejoice, be glad and give thanks. *–St. Paul*

GRACE UNDER FIRE

Inner serenity and faith are reflected outward as graceful composure and poise.

Grace is evident in successes, or in the face of life's inevitable difficulties and painful experiences.

GRACE IS ABSENCE OF EVERYTHING INDICATING PAIN OR DIFFICULTY, HESITATION OR INCONGRUITY.
–William Hazlitt

NUGGET OF HOPE

Inner spirituality and peace are the passageway and reservoir of inner tranquillity and Hope that appear outwardly, as grace under fire.

REACHING OUT

To find comfort from pain and loss, reach within–and then reach out
to those who love you and care about your struggle and well being.
This includes family members, special friends and co-workers– those
who create The Family Culture.

ALL THE FLOWERS OF ALL THE
TOMORROWS ARE IN THE
SEEDS OF TODAY.
–*Chinese Proverb*

Each member of The Family Culture
says take my hand, stand on my shoulders, you are my brother and
sister and together, we can. Those who believe in and live The
Family Culture know, Divine Love expressed through humans is the
seed of mass epidemics of hope.

NUGGET OF HOPE
The welfare of each is bound up in the welfare of all. *–Helen Keller*

COMFORTING OTHERS

In our difficulties, we can learn to identify with others' pain.

And then, we can comfort others in their times of pain, giving them hope, pleasing our maker and creating a legacy of love.

GOD DOES NOT COMFORT US TO MAKE US COMFORTABLE. BUT TO MAKE US COMFORTERS
—John Henry Jowett

NUGGET OF HOPE

I used to ask God to help me. Then I asked if I might help Him. I ended up by asking Him to do His work through me. *—Hudson Taylor*

EXPRESSING LOVE

Love is the centerpiece of Eternal Truth and the wellspring of personal and relationship well being. It is the most enduring power and is available in unlimited portions.

Choosing to openly express our love is wise–a most honorable and hopeful gift that says "I recognize, encourage and feel blessed to nurture others and their uniqueness and specialness."

And, each experience fills hearts deeper with love and compassion that make our world a far better place, one safer and more secure for all.

YOU WILL FIND, AS YOU LOOK BACK UPON YOUR LIFE, THAT THE MOMENTS WHEN YOU REALLY LIVED ARE THE MOMENTS WHEN YOU HAVE DONE THINGS IN THE SPIRIT OF LOVE.
–*Henry Drummond*

NUGGET OF HOPE
The soft touch of love expressed leaves an abiding imprint of hope, in us and others.

LOVING
WITHOUT LIMITS

Unconditional love is the wellspring of the best we have and the
key that opens the door to life's greatest satisfaction.

The best love is the love we give.

Uncover the wellspring, open the door
and find that loving without limits restores dreams and hopes and
yields excellence.

NUGGET OF HOPE
The petals of the flower of limitless loving are unconditional giving and sharing.

PART TWO

I'M LIVING JUST AS THE
CENTURY ENDS.

A GREAT LEAF, THAT GOD
AND YOU AND I HAVE
COVERED WITH WRITING
TURNS NOW, OVERHEAD,
IN STRANGE HANDS. WE
FEEL THE SWEEP
OF IT LIKE A WIND.

WE SEE THE BRIGHTNESS
OF A NEW PAGE WHERE
EVERYTHING YET CAN
HAPPEN...

—Rainer Maria Rilke

Step forward into your Bright & Blessed Future!

UNSEEN POWER

A wise woman who was traveling in the mountains found a precious stone in a stream. The next day she met another traveler who was hungry, and the wise woman opened her bag to share her food. The hungry traveler saw the precious stone and asked the woman to give it to him. She did so without hesitation. The traveler left, rejoicing in his good fortune. He knew the stone was worth enough to give him security for a lifetime.

But a few days later, he came back to return the stone to the wise woman. "I've been thinking," he said, "I know how valuable the stone is, but I give it back in the hope you can give me something even more precious. Give me what you have within you that enabled you to give me the stone."

The Wise Woman's Stone
–Author Unknown

LETTING GO

Letting go of the past is hard to do. We all hold our experiences close to our hearts and sometimes long to bring them back. But, as Debbie says, the past is like a match that burned brightly, then slowly faded out until it glowed only in memory. She goes on to share this wisdom and inspiration.

We grow from our experiences, and we learn many wise lessons from past events. But we live in the present, and there's a light on today.

IF WE CONTINUE TO MOURN THE PAST, WE FORGET TO LIVE IN THE PRESENT, AND THE FUTURE BECOMES LIKE A BURNED-OUT MATCH, THE WIND CARRYING ITS SMOKE INTO OBLIVION.
–Debbie Guthery

Bring your pictures, your memories, and your passions with you. Visit the ones that make you smile or bring you wisdom. Set the others silently upon the smoke, for the wind to carry them away.

NUGGET OF HOPE

To grow, we must heal and to heal, we must let go.

BEGINNINGS

There's always a best way of doing everything.

So it is, with beginnings.

LIFE MUST BE UNDERSTOOD
BACKWARDS: BUT... IT MUST
BE LIVED FORWARDS.
—*Søren Kierkegaard*

Begin by looking back, reflecting, and then looking forward.

Begin with the best in heart and mind.

Begin with a faith that looks for the good, the value, and the promise in others and all situations.

Hopeful desires, thoughts and attitudes lead to the best results.

NUGGET OF HOPE

A journey of a thousand miles begins with a single step. —*Chinese Proverb*

HIGH EXPECTATIONS

Real security results from being certain about eternal matters.

Certain of those, we have highest expectations.

HIGH EXPECTATIONS
ARE THE KEY TO
EVERYTHING.
—Sam Walton

Highest faith is being certain of The Divine. That confidence is the basis of a higher viewpoint of life where only the very best is expected, now and into eternity.

NUGGET OF HOPE

For I believe in harbors at the end. *—Thomas Fuller*

DON'T WORRY. HAVE FAITH.

Consider this poem from Debbie Guthery.

Bright are her eyes my little girl faith
*   her timing soft her presence like lace*
She appears in a whisper as one believes
*   and captures a moment sometimes hard to conceive.*
She clears all the darkness that hides passion's light
*   and shows us a way through the darkest nights*
So subtle her spirit, so strong is her hold
*   believing is simple with faith to behold.*

Saying don't worry, have faith, is easier said than done. Right?

How can you be at peace, free of anxiety?

BY BELIEVING IN ROSES, ONE
BRINGS THEM TO BLOOM.
—French Proverb

The Bible is clear that we are to give the cares of
life to God, in faith through prayer. By give, I mean in prayer time, release your
worries to The Divine and go your way in faith, knowing your concerns are in the
most skilled hands in the universe.

Another promise on the pages of Wisdom is that God always works out everything
for good to those who are in harmonious, personal relationship and partnership
with The Divine. It may not turn out the way we thought it should, but The
Divine promises it will be good for all concerned. So, as you pray and daily release
worries to God, stand steadfast in faith on that promise.

Faith and worry are incompatible. Worry negates faith and vice versa. If you worry, you destroy the single-minded concentration it takes to follow Wisdom's instructions on faith, prayer and making choices based on the principles, values and priorities of Eternal Truth.

I would be remiss if I didn't mention two additional thoughts on worry. First, we often worry over things that never could reasonably occur. Other times, we worry because we know the choices we have made and the actions we have taken were unwise. Many respond to the distress by manipulating others and by behaviors that create problems or compound problems caused by unwise choices. Worry will not change a choice already made. Accompanied by unwise behavior, worry only assures things go from bad to worse.

Instead of worrying or remaining anxious about anything, my suggestions are fivefold.
1. Read the Bible every day.
2. Release your concerns and cares to God through prayer, which begins with thanksgiving.
3. Have faith in The Divine, believe that God works things out for good in His time and receive the peace of God that comes on the wings of those type prayers.
4. As you wait in faith, take St. Paul's advice. Think on things that are good, noble and pure.
5. Make spiritually wise choices.

NUGGET OF HOPE
Picture the beauty of roses in faith. Wisdom plants them, Honor waters them, and Hope comes back, soaks in, and enjoys their beauty and fragrance.

TIME

Our life is currency we can spend only once.

Soak time in.

Ride its winds, go with its flow.

Enjoy every moment of time.

NUGGET OF HOPE

Teach us to number our days, realize how few they are and spend each wisely.
–King David

PEACE AND HAPPINESS

When we accept the true spiritual nature of our destiny, our trials and times of confusion or despair can only temporarily cloak our inner state of peace and happiness.

Inner peace is the basis of genuinely lasting happiness.

NUGGET OF HOPE
THE SIMPLE PATH
The fruit of silence is PRAYER.
The fruit of prayer is FAITH.
The fruit of faith is LOVE.
The fruit of love is SERVICE.
The fruit of service is PEACE.
–Mother Teresa

WE HAVE A RIGHT TO BE HAPPY AND PEACEFUL. WE HAVE BEEN CREATED FOR THIS—WE ARE BORN TO BE HAPPY—AND WE CAN ONLY FIND TRUE HAPPINESS AND PEACE WHEN WE ARE IN LOVE WITH GOD.
–Mother Teresa

FULFILLMENT

We each are co-creators of our life, choosing our direction.

Disillusionment can be the gateway of the most
important frontier of life: Spiritual Awakening.

At that gate, we can change our direction and choose to discover
our Divine potential–pursuing a higher
purpose and moving towards genuine fulfillment.

NUGGET OF HOPE

Let each become all that they were created capable of being.
–Thomas Carlyle

DREAMS DO COME TRUE.

Dream a while, release your worries, face your fears, bare your soul and open wide your spirit to Hope and a bright, better future.

Remember these wise words from Albert Einstein, "The gift of fantasy has meant more to me than any talent for abstract, positive thinking."

ALL OUR DREAMS CAN COME TRUE, IF WE HAVE THE COURAGE TO PURSUE THEM.
—Walt Disney

NUGGET OF HOPE

If our dreams are honorable and spiritually born, we dream wisely and insure our success, as we continue to allow God's partnership along our path of life.

DAWNING OF
A NEW DAY

We are responsible for our life—as it
is, as it should be and
as it is to be.

FOR THE MIND DISTURBED, THE
STILL BEAUTY OF DAWN IS
NATURE'S FINEST BALM.
—*Edwin Teale*

James Baldwin said, "Not everything that is faced can be
changed. But nothing can be changed until it is faced."

So, for the rest of today, face what needs changing. Look inside,
do an honest accounting and write down the unwise things that
have caused you to fall short of your best.

At dawn tomorrow, leave the past behind, get into the future
changing what can be changed living truth, nothing but truth,
so help you God.

NUGGET OF HOPE

We turn, not older with years, but newer every day. —Emily Dickinson

BECOMING ANEW

Begin every day by connecting with The Divine Spirit,
to renew your soul.

Close your eyes, listen to your heart... and remember.

Speak--pray--to The Divine who has created you.

Reconnect and become anew.

NUGGET OF HOPE

The exceptional life is the one connected at the heart to The Divine.

REVERENCE

I often dream of You,

> as You dip Your brush into the many colors of the world
>> and stroke it so delicately against the bluest skies,
>>> filling them with pastels.

> As You dip Your brush again,
>> You release a fragrance of pines, rain, and honeysuckle.

I savor all that You offer,

> and I am humbled that I may be the guest
>> of Your silent design.

—Debbie Guthery

FOR YOU ALONE,
LORD GOD, ARE
WORTHY OF OUR
WORSHIP.
—St. John

NUGGET OF HOPE

I worship You, You are worthy of my highest praise, for in You, Lord God, there is Real HOPE.

BREATHING IN

Embrace the nourishment of Divine Wisdom. Breathe in the purity
of Eternal Truth, inhaling its peace and Hope.

Wisdom, Truth and The Spirit of God within continually satisfy
and quench our deepest hunger and thirst, sus-
tain our lives in the deserts and storms of life
and impart to us the faith, courage, strength,
confidence and Hope to guide us to the brighter days
of a sure future.

> WISDOM IS TO THE SOUL
> WHAT HEALTH IS TO
> THE BODY.
> *–François de La Rochefoucauld*

NUGGET OF HOPE
Allowing The Divine Spirit to guide us by Wisdom and Truth protects us
and brings highest prosperity.

AWAKEN YOUR SPIRIT!

Blind from birth, Helen Keller was suddenly awakened, spiritually.

On the most important frontier of life, she welcomed the light, joy and freedom that truth rewards all whom discover and embrace it. Instantly, her Hope was elevated and her confidence soared.

> I KNEW THAT "W-A-T-E-R" MEANT THIS WONDER-FUL COOL SOMETHING THAT WAS FLOWING OVER MY HAND. THAT LIVING WATER AWAK-ENED MY SOUL, GAVE IT LIGHT, JOY, SET IT FREE!
> *–Helen Keller*

This story of true greatness inspires and gives us all great Hope and confidence about our lives and the future.

NUGGET OF HOPE

With the inner sunshine of Eternal Truth as our life light and line of vision, we never lose sight of our highest aspirations and wisely move each day toward them. We pursue our higher purpose and become all we were created capable of being.

FEEL YOUR SPIRIT!

Valuable change is inside out.

Attaining an intimate, inner personal
relationship with The Divine will move your life
upward to highest significance.

NUGGET OF HOPE

Give me beauty in the inward soul; may the outward and the inward
be at one. —*Socrates*

THERE IS ONE
SPECTACLE
GRANDER THAN
ANY SKY, THAT IS
THE INTERIOR OF
THE SOUL.
—*Victor Hugo*

INSIDE JOB

The way we are inside counts the most.

Truth opens your eyes to new Beauty and your ears to new Music.

Truth releases you to a heightened reality of meaning and Hope.

Recognize and be filled with Truth when you hear it. This will bring you wisdom.

Believe on that Truth through faith. This will bring you Real Hope.

Act on that Truth. This will bring you peace and joy.

NUGGET OF HOPE

Some things you can count, don't really count. Some things you cannot count, really count. *–Albert Einstein*

HIGHEST INSIGHT

Valuable experience is the result of living out our faith in The Divine.

That experience builds our faith–not faith in experience or ourselves, but in the One who made the mountain and the paths up and down it.

NUGGET OF HOPE

God's thoughts and ways are higher than ours are, as far as heaven is above earth. –*The Prophet Isaiah*

COMPASS OF TRUTH

Honor shapes the inner person with a diligence and discipline that frees the heart and mind to soar–without regret, compromise, or doubt.

Living Eternal Truth is the best way to assure we live with Honor, that our lives count for what really counts. Eternal Truth as our guide, we have the foundation of Honor needed to shape a life based on important values.

TRUTH IS NOT A CRYSTAL THAT YOU CAN STASH AWAY IN YOUR POCKET. IT IS AN INFINITE LIQUID INTO WHICH YOU FALL.
–*Robert von Musil*

Living Eternal Truth, our inner spirit person is guided by Divine Wisdom, Honor and Hope. Those are the qualities marking one who not only dreams big, but also dreams wisely from a honorable heart. They attain True Greatness. What has eternal worth is their life's defining goal.

NUGGET OF HOPE

Guided by the principles, values and priorities of Eternal Truth, we can achieve the best and inspire the same in lives we touch.

DIVINE WISDOM

Ultimate Wisdom and True Greatness begins with the realization—through a lifetime of study, a moment of blinding enlightenment, a period of soulful, reflective prayer—that the greatest giver we can emulate is The Divine Creator.

True Wisdom begins
- with the realization that the material
  has no value in the long run.
- with the realization that life is a gift.
- with gratitude and respect for this gift.
- with gratitude and respect for the Giver.
- with gratitude and respect for all other life.
- when one decides to emulate givers and not merely
  have a hand held out for receiving.

Wisdom enables us—with guidance and tools for decision making. It awakens the heart and instructs the inner person to know what is right and motivate it to do right.

Wisdom ennobles us—with compassion, thoughtfulness and generosity. Applied to daily living and working, it has profound positive effects in the heart of our inner lives and outwardly, in our role and relationship conduct.

NUGGET OF HOPE

Guided by Wisdom, we discover life's greatest Hope and attain highest prosperity.

LIFT YOUR EYES!

Looking up reveals a brighter, better future.

Keeping our gaze upward,
fixed and steady, we can be
sure with God's great help we
can do anything.

BE GLAD OF LIFE BECAUSE IT
GIVES YOU THE CHANCE TO LOVE
AND TO WORK AND TO PLAY AND
TO LOOK UP AT THE STARS.
–Henry Van Dyke

Looking up daily, we can be led safely along the path to the far
horizon and the realization of today's dreams and deepest hopes.

NUGGET OF HOPE

I will lift my eyes to the hills of heaven, where my strength and help comes
from. *–King David*

TAKE FLIGHT!

Accept and express God's loving kindness, mercy, justice, honor and humility, inspiration and hope.

Dare to reach inside to discover all your God-given potential and travel this better path. Discover your eagles' wings and use them and the power and knowledge within, to soar to new heights.

GOD HAS GIVEN YOU A SPIRIT WITH WINGS ON WHICH TO SOAR INTO THE SPACIOUS FIRMAMENT OF LOVE AND FREEDOM.
—*Kahlil Gibran*

NUGGET OF HOPE

Connected to and inspired and guided by The Divine within, we are eagles, able to fly above clouds and life's storms and soar to make our highest dreams and hopes reality.

YOU MATTER.

You are enough.

Lives that most powerfully influence are perfectly simple. These individuals recognize and nurture each person as a single piece of an infinite puzzle, a very unique, special part of the whole tapestry of life.

YOUR SOLE CONTRIBUTION TO THE SUM OF THINGS IS YOURSELF.
–Frank Crane

Keeping our lives simple gives us time to plant, water and come back to enjoy roses of Hope.

NUGGET OF HOPE

Do ordinary things with extraordinary love. *–Mother Teresa*

MAKING WISE HABITS

We fall into unwise habits, heart first and then, head over heels.

Habits spring from the food of thought fed our spirit an models we mimic. Consider this thought food, as models for making better habits:

- Rest your mind and body.
- Nourish your soul.
- Have faith in God.
- Base your dreams on Truth.
- Place your hope in God.
- Love without limits.
- Give, share, and forgive, without strings.
- In all matters, live Honor guided by Wisdom.
- Don't forget to breathe!

NUGGET OF HOPE

As we think in our heart, so are we. *–King Solomon*

OFFERING THE OLIVE BRANCH

A spiritually wise heart leads us, promptly and willingly, to account for our mistakes and injustices. It also causes us to realize that forgiveness is the work of The Divine.

We have to choose to let the other person off the hook and work out a way to get along with that person. It's as simple as that, or it's as complex and destructive as unforgiveness can be. Wisdom inside us will enable us to develop the self-discipline to be forgiving. We can accomplish much more with forgiveness than with bitterness and resentment. True resolution of conflict can happen only when unconditional love reigns in our hearts.

FORGIVENESS IS AN ACT OF THE WILL, AND THE WILL CAN FUNCTION REGARDLESS OF THE TEMPERATURE OF THE HEART.
—*Corrie Ten Boom*

Healing relationships starts with forgiveness. Saying we're sorry and truly meaning it, requires taking initiative and making amends, never repeating the offense again and forgetting it, if we were the one offending or offended.

When I was a boy, my maternal grandfather, Papa Adcock, once banned my father from Papa's home for what seemed like a trivial reason. After weeks of not seeing our entire family, Papa walked more than five miles to our house, apologized, and asked forgiveness. He went home a happy man, leaving behind a happy family who immediately resumed daily visits to Papa's home.

What do Papa's actions tell us about Wisdom? When we forgive Wisdom's way, we become instruments of healing.

Learn today to forgive–Wisdom's way. When The Divine within inspires us, we choose to make amends and achieve reconciliation. Then, we can let the past sleep, so the future can awaken! Allowing God to work within us, we can initiate limitless forgiveness, make amends, restore, heal, and effect true reconciliation.

NUGGET OF HOPE

To the degree within your control, live peaceably with all. –*St. Paul*

KEEPING PROMISES

When you live according to the Wisdom imparted to you and through you, you live with Honor—an old fashioned word with powerful, eternal relevance.

Honor takes that Wisdom and habitually puts it into action. Sound character is formed. With Eternal Truth as the spirit person's ethical standard, Honor becomes the interior lifestyle that outwardly is seen as integrity beyond reproach. When Honor thrives in our lives, it takes hold in every personal and work-related role and relationship, yielding excellence.

Society rests on the integrity of every individual—and promises made being kept. Promises broken lead to the death of a society and the individual member, no matter how materially prosperous or skilled they may be. When reliability of promises goes, our hope and everything else goes.

> NOBODY CAN CONTRIBUTE TO THE BEST OF HUMANITY WHO DOES NOT MAKE THE BEST OUT OF HIMSELF.
> —Johann Gottfried Herder

A promise is a promise. Size or cost of fulfillment matters not.

NUGGET OF HOPE

It is wise, honorable and hopeful to be true to promises. No matter what.

LISTENING TO YOUR HEART

The most productive interpretation of life is through a childlike heart.

A child's heart is innocent and pure and sees life's best and extraordinary.
By tuning out the chatter of the head and meditating on the insightful
messages of our childlike heart, we make
wise choices that stand the test of time.

IT IS ONLY WITH THE HEART
ONE CAN SEE RIGHTLY. WHAT
IS ESSENTIAL IS INVISIBLE TO
THE EYE.
—*Antoine de Saint-Exupéry*

NUGGET OF HOPE

Be still, rest your mind, keep your heart pure, listen to its childlike innocence,
find the peace within undisturbed by worry and breathe in the tranquillity
and strength.

LIGHTING SHINING STARS

Adult models are primary ways children learn to be adults.
Most powerful among those is personal example of parents. Living
models of truth reveal God to our children and mold their heart
and mind so they can be Shining Stars lighting up their world with
hope, kindness, honor, dependability, and love.

We need to begin by seeing newborns as The Divine sees them.
Each new child is unique, a very special Shining Star in God's eyes.
Unqualified uniqueness and nearly limitless potential live in every
child. When we recognize, encourage, and nurture the uniqueness
of every child, we give them roots to dig deep and wings to soar
high and land safely. The truly wise adopt that view and never, ever
change it. They seek to provide roots and
wings and teach children to listen to the
beat of that different drummer, allowing
God's purpose for their life to be fulfilled.

CHILDREN ARE THE LIVING
MESSAGES WE SEND TO A
TIME WE WILL NOT SEE.
—*Neil Postman*

With roots and wings, our children have a strong sense of who they are and the power to take them to the places they were created to go. Then, these Shining Stars soar, see bright horizons, and land safely as they pursue their grandest dreams.

N U G G E T S   O F   H O P E

Children are the hands by which we take hold of heaven.
–*Henry Ward Beeche*

My hope for my children must be that they respond to the still, small voice of God in their own hearts.
 –*Andrew Young*

MAKING PROGRESS

Dedication to purpose is the power behind true progress–advancements in relationships and the welfare of mankind–that stands the test of time.

NUGGET OF HOPE

The only true measure of success is the ratio between what we might have done and what we might have been on the one hand, and the thing we have made and the thing we have made of ourselves on the other.
–H.G. Wells

THE TEST OF OUR PROGRESS IS NOT WHETHER WE ADD MORE TO THE ABUNDANCE OF THOSE WHO HAVE MUCH: IT IS WHETHER WE PRO- VIDE ENOUGH FOR THOSE WHO HAVE TOO LITTLE.
–Franklin Roosevelt

CELEBRATING LIFE

Dance on the clouds, gleefully rejoice, sing and make music, celebrate life!

Garrison Keillor said, "Thank you God, for this good life and forgive us if we do not love it enough."

Human life, what a wonderful gift! Celebrate it. Praise the Giver. Have a grand adventure! Maybe you'll get a little wet or hurt, maybe you won't be safe from life's "slings and arrows" but you will be truly living.

By living every moment as a special one, we enjoy it, today, tomorrow and store up benefits in eternity.

NUGGET OF HOPE
Our life is a gift from God. What we do with it is our gift back.

DIVINE HOPE

Real Hope is God shining through you. It lifts you and sustains you and at the same time lifts and sustains others.

The confidence, security and assurance you possess, by walking in faith with The God of Hope, activates your current and future dreams and expectations–and illuminates, blesses and motivates others to seek this Light.

HOPE IS A THING
WITH FEATHERS
THAT PERCHES
ON THE SOUL,
AND SINGS
THE TUNE WITH-
OUT WORDS,
AND NEVER
STOPS AT ALL.
–Emily Dickinson

Take down walls, uncover your heart's eyes, see and move to your higher destiny. Hold onto your dreams and hopes. Never give up. Realize it takes time for them to become reality. Believe. Let faith carry you, as you soar in flight. See your Hope become reality.

NUGGET OF HOPE

Tucked deep within our heart, Divine Hope gets us through the storms and tragedies of life, renews our soul, restores its hope and assures our dreams are recaptured and realized.